The Radiance of H Journey to Inner Joy

Chapter 1: The Power of Positive Thinking

In the bustling corridors of our lives, it's easy to be swept away by the currents of negativity. Yet, amidst this whirlwind, there lies a transformative power within our thoughts. This chapter explores the science behind positive thinking, illustrating how a shift in our mental landscape can lead to profound changes in our overall well-being.

Chapter 2: Cultivating Gratitude

Gratitude is the heartbeat of happiness. Here, we delve into practices that help us recognize and appreciate the small joys that often go unnoticed. From daily gratitude journaling to mindfulness exercises, discover how cultivating a sense of thankfulness can elevate your mood and perspective.

Chapter 3: Embracing the Present Moment

Our minds often wander into the past or future, missing the richness of the present moment. This chapter guides you through techniques to anchor yourself in the now, helping you savour life's experiences and find joy in everyday occurrences.

Chapter 4: The Art of Positive Affirmations

Words have a powerful impact on our reality. Learn how to craft and use positive affirmations to rewire your thought patterns and reinforce a more optimistic outlook. Real-life examples and exercises will empower you to create affirmations that resonate with your personal goals.

Chapter 5: Nurturing Relationships

Human connections play a crucial role in our happiness. Explore how to build and maintain healthy relationships, practice empathy, and engage in meaningful interactions. This chapter provides strategies for fostering deeper connections and creating a supportive social network.

Chapter 6: Finding Joy in Creativity

Creativity is a wellspring of joy and self-expression. Discover how engaging in creative activities, whether it's painting, writing, or cooking, can serve as a joyful outlet and a means of personal fulfilment. Find inspiration and practical tips to integrate creativity into your daily life.

Chapter 7: The Role of Self-Care

Self-care is not a luxury but a necessity for maintaining mental and emotional health. This chapter outlines various self-care practices, from physical exercise to relaxation techniques, that can help you recharge and cultivate a more positive mindset.

Chapter 8: Overcoming Challenges with a Positive Mindset

Life is filled with ups and downs, but maintaining a positive mindset can help you navigate through challenges more effectively. Learn strategies for overcoming adversity and turning setbacks into opportunities for growth and resilience.

Chapter 9: Creating a Joyful Environment

Our surroundings influence our mood and outlook. Explore ways to create an environment that fosters happiness, from organising your space to incorporating elements that bring you joy. This chapter offers practical tips for designing a living space that reflects and enhances your inner positivity.

Chapter 10: Spreading Joy to Others

True happiness often comes from giving. Discover the profound impact of acts of kindness, volunteering, and supporting others. This chapter highlights how spreading joy can enrich your own life and create a ripple effect of positivity in the world.

Chapter 11: Embracing a Life of Joy

As we conclude our journey, reflect on the practices and insights shared throughout the book. Embrace the idea that happiness is not a destination but a continuous journey. This final chapter encourages you to integrate these principles into your life and live each day with a heart full of joy.

Appendices

- Daily Reflection Worksheet Guided prompts for journaling your thoughts and tracking your progress.
- Resource List Recommended books, apps, and websites for further exploration of positive thinking and happiness.
- Inspirational Quotes A collection of quotes to uplift and inspire you on your journey to a joyful life.

In The Radiance of Happy Thoughts: A Journey to Inner Joy," you'll find a blend of practical advice, inspiring stories, and actionable strategies to help you cultivate a happier and more fulfilling life. Dive in, embrace the power of positive thinking, and let the radiance of happy thoughts illuminate your path.

Chapter: 1 The Power of Positive Thinking

In a world brimming with challenges and uncertainties, the concept of positive thinking emerges as a beacon of hope and resilience. It is often said that our thoughts shape our reality, and this sentiment lies at the heart of the philosophy of positive thinking. But what exactly does it mean to think positively, and how can it influence our lives in profound ways? In this chapter, we will explore the transformative power of positive thinking, its impact on our mental and physical well-being, and practical strategies to harness its benefits.

Understanding Positive Thinking

Positive thinking involves more than merely adopting an optimistic outlook on life. It is a conscious choice to focus on the favourable aspects of any situation, even when faced with adversity. This mindset doesn't ignore the difficulties we encounter but instead encourages us to approach them with a constructive attitude.

At its core, positive thinking is about shifting our perspective from problems to possibilities. When we train our minds to seek out the good in every experience, we open ourselves up to a world of opportunities and solutions that might otherwise remain hidden. It's a mental framework that allows us to cope with stress, build resilience, and cultivate a sense of well-being.

The Science Behind Positive Thinking

Research in psychology and neuroscience has shed light on how positive thinking influences our brains and bodies. One of the most significant findings is the relationship between positivity and overall health. Studies have shown that individuals with a positive outlook are more likely to experience lower levels of stress, reduced risk of chronic illnesses, and improved immune function.

The brain's neuroplasticity plays a crucial role in this process. Neuroplasticity refers to the brain's ability to reorganise itself by forming new neural connections throughout life. Positive thinking can contribute to this reorganisation, reinforcing pathways associated with happiness and well-being. When we consistently engage in positive thought patterns, we strengthen neural circuits that promote optimism and resilience.

Additionally, positive thinking has been linked to the release of neurochemicals such as dopamine and serotonin, which are associated with feelings of pleasure and contentment. These chemical changes not only improve our mood but also enhance our overall quality of life.

The Benefits of Positive Thinking

The impact of positive thinking extends far beyond our mental health. Here are several key benefits that underscore its significance:

1. **Enhanced Resilience:** Positive thinkers are better equipped to handle setbacks and challenges. By maintaining a hopeful outlook, they are more likely to persevere and find solutions, rather than giving up in the face of adversity.
2. **Improved Relationships:** A positive attitude can strengthen relationships by fostering better communication, empathy,

and mutual support. Positivity is contagious, and when we approach others with a positive mindset, we often receive the same in return.
3. **Greater Success:** Research suggests that positive thinking can enhance performance and success. Individuals who believe in their abilities are more likely to set ambitious goals, take proactive steps, and achieve their desired outcomes.
4. **Increased Well-Being:** A positive mindset contributes to overall well-being by reducing stress, improving mood, and fostering a sense of fulfilment. It promotes a healthier lifestyle and encourages self-care practices.
5. **Longevity:** Studies have found that individuals with a positive outlook on life tend to live longer. This may be attributed to their healthier lifestyle choices, better stress management, and overall enhanced well-being.

Cultivating a Positive Mindset

Developing a positive mindset is a gradual process that involves conscious effort and practice. Here are some strategies to help you cultivate and maintain positive thinking:

1. **Practice Gratitude:** Keeping a gratitude journal can help shift your focus from what's lacking to what's abundant in your life. Regularly noting things you're thankful for can enhance your mood and foster a more positive outlook.
2. **Challenge Negative Thoughts:** When you catch yourself thinking negatively, pause and challenge those thoughts. Ask yourself whether they are based on facts or assumptions, and consider alternative, more positive perspectives.
3. **Surround Yourself with Positivity:** The people and environments you interact with can influence your mindset. Surround yourself with supportive, uplifting individuals and seek out positive, inspiring experiences.

4. **Engage in Positive Self-Talk:** Replace self-critical thoughts with affirmations and encouragement. Positive self-talk can boost your confidence and reinforce a more optimistic view of yourself and your abilities.
5. **Set Realistic Goals:** Setting and achieving small, manageable goals can provide a sense of accomplishment and reinforce your positive mindset. Celebrate your successes and use them as motivation for future endeavours.
6. **Practice Mindfulness and Meditation:** Mindfulness and meditation practices can help you stay present and focused, reducing the impact of negative thoughts and fostering a more positive outlook. Regular practice can enhance your ability to manage stress and maintain emotional balance.
7. **Seek Professional Support:** If negative thinking patterns are deeply ingrained or causing significant distress, consider seeking support from a mental health professional. Therapy can provide valuable tools and techniques for transforming negative thought patterns and building resilience.

Overcoming Challenges with Positive Thinking

While positive thinking offers numerous benefits, it is essential to recognize that it does not mean ignoring reality or pretending that everything is perfect. Challenges and difficulties are an inevitable part of life, and a positive mindset is not about denying these experiences but rather about how we respond to them.

When facing significant obstacles, it's important to balance positivity with practical problem-solving. Positive thinking can help you approach challenges with optimism and creativity, but addressing the root causes of problems and taking proactive steps is equally crucial.

Additionally, practising self-compassion is vital. Being kind to yourself during difficult times and acknowledging your struggles can help you maintain a positive mindset without falling into the trap of unrealistic expectations or self-criticism.

Conclusion

The power of positive thinking lies in its ability to transform our perspective and enhance our overall well-being. By focusing on the positive aspects of life, we can build resilience, strengthen relationships, and improve our health and happiness. Cultivating a positive mindset involves conscious effort and practice, but the rewards are profound and far-reaching.

As you embark on your journey toward a more positive outlook, remember that it is a continuous process. Embrace the challenges and opportunities along the way, and trust in the transformative power of your thoughts. By choosing to see the good in every situation and nurturing a mindset of positivity, you can unlock your full potential and lead a more fulfilling, joyful life.

Chapter: 2 Cultivating Gratitude

In an age of constant striving and perpetual busyness, the simple act of cultivating gratitude can be a profound antidote to stress and dissatisfaction. Gratitude, the practice of recognizing and appreciating the positives in our lives, holds the power to transform our emotional well-being and enhance our overall quality of life. This chapter delves into the essence of gratitude, its benefits, and practical strategies for incorporating it into our daily routines.

Understanding Gratitude

Gratitude is more than just saying "thank you" when someone does something nice for us. It's a deep-seated acknowledgment of the good things in our lives, whether they come from people, experiences, or circumstances. At its core, gratitude involves a recognition of what we have and an appreciation for the contributions of others and the larger world.

Gratitude is often described as a complex emotion that involves a sense of thankfulness and an acknowledgment of the value in what we receive. It encompasses both an emotional experience and a cognitive process. When we feel grateful, we not only experience positive emotions but also engage in a mental shift that allows us to recognize and cherish the good aspects of our lives.

The Science Behind Gratitude

Recent research has provided compelling evidence of the benefits of gratitude on our mental and physical health. Studies have shown that practising gratitude can lead to increased happiness, reduced stress, and improved overall well-being. Here are some key findings from the science of gratitude:

1. **Enhanced Mental Health:** Grateful individuals tend to experience lower levels of depression and anxiety. Gratitude practices can shift our focus from negative thoughts to positive ones, reducing feelings of sadness and fostering a more optimistic outlook.
2. **Improved Physical Health:** Research suggests that grateful people often report better physical health. They are more likely to engage in healthy behaviors such as regular exercise and balanced nutrition. Gratitude can also reduce symptoms of illness and improve sleep quality.

3. **Stronger Relationships:** Gratitude can strengthen relationships by promoting positive interactions and increasing feelings of connection. Expressing appreciation to others enhances social bonds and encourages reciprocal acts of kindness.
4. **Increased Resilience:** Gratitude helps individuals cope with challenges and setbacks. By focusing on what they have rather than what they lack, grateful people are better equipped to handle stress and adversity.
5. **Greater Life Satisfaction:** Cultivating gratitude can lead to greater life satisfaction. By recognizing and appreciating the good things in life, individuals are more likely to feel content and fulfilled.

Practical Strategies for Cultivating Gratitude

Cultivating gratitude is a practice that can be integrated into daily life through various techniques. Here are some effective strategies to help you develop and maintain a gratitude practice:

1. **Gratitude Journaling:** One of the most popular and effective methods for cultivating gratitude is keeping a gratitude journal. Set aside a few minutes each day to write down three to five things you are grateful for. These can be small, everyday occurrences or significant life events. Regular journaling helps shift your focus from what's lacking to what's abundant.
2. **Gratitude Letters:** Writing letters of appreciation to people who have had a positive impact on your life can be a powerful exercise. Expressing your gratitude in writing not only benefits the recipient but also reinforces your own feelings of thankfulness. You don't always have to send the letter—sometimes the act of writing it is enough.
3. **Mindful Appreciation:** Incorporate moments of mindful appreciation into your daily routine. Take a few minutes each day to reflect on the positive aspects of your life. This could be during a quiet moment, while enjoying a cup of coffee, or

before going to sleep. Allow yourself to fully experience and savor the feelings of gratitude.
4. **Gratitude Rituals:** Create rituals that incorporate gratitude into your daily life. For example, you might start each meal by expressing thanks for the food and the people who contributed to it. Or you could end each day by reflecting on one positive experience and expressing gratitude for it.
5. **Visual Reminders:** Place visual reminders of gratitude around your living space. This could include inspirational quotes, photographs, or objects that remind you of positive experiences. These reminders can serve as prompts to reflect on the things you are grateful for throughout the day.
6. **Gratitude Meditation:** Incorporate gratitude into your meditation practice. Begin your meditation session by focusing on things you are grateful for. This can help set a positive tone for the meditation and reinforce your feelings of appreciation.
7. **Acts of Kindness:** Engage in acts of kindness and generosity. Helping others and contributing to their well-being can enhance your own sense of gratitude. Whether it's volunteering, offering support to a friend, or simply being considerate, acts of kindness can create a ripple effect of positivity and appreciation.
8. **Gratitude and Challenges:** Use challenging situations as opportunities to practise gratitude. When facing difficulties, try to find aspects of the situation for which you can be thankful. This practice can help reframe your perspective and make it easier to cope with adversity.

Overcoming Barriers to Gratitude

While cultivating gratitude offers numerous benefits, it can sometimes be challenging to maintain, especially during difficult times. Here are some common barriers to gratitude and strategies to overcome them:

1. **Negativity Bias:** Our brains have a natural tendency to focus on negative experiences more than positive ones. To counteract this bias, actively seek out and acknowledge positive experiences. Regular gratitude practices, such as journaling and mindfulness, can help shift your focus from negativity to appreciation.
2. **Comparison:** Comparing ourselves to others can undermine feelings of gratitude. Instead of focusing on what others have that you don't, concentrate on your own unique blessings and achievements. Practising gratitude for your own experiences can help reduce feelings of envy and inadequacy.
3. **Routine and Complacency:** Gratitude practices can sometimes become routine, leading to complacency. To keep your practice fresh and meaningful, vary your gratitude exercises and explore new ways to express appreciation. This can help maintain your enthusiasm and deepen your sense of gratitude.
4. **Lack of Time:** Busy schedules can make it challenging to prioritise gratitude practices. Set aside dedicated time each day for gratitude exercises, even if it's just a few minutes. Incorporate gratitude into existing routines, such as mealtimes or bedtime, to ensure it becomes a regular part of your life.
5. **Emotional Resistance:** Some individuals may find it difficult to feel grateful during times of personal struggle or emotional pain. Acknowledge your feelings and allow yourself to experience them fully. Gradually incorporate gratitude practices, focusing on small, manageable aspects of your life that you can appreciate.

The Ripple Effect of Gratitude

The practice of gratitude extends beyond personal well-being and can have a profound impact on the wider world. When we cultivate gratitude, we not only enhance our own lives but also contribute to a more positive and connected community. Acts of kindness, appreciation, and generosity create a ripple effect, inspiring others to adopt similar practices and fostering a culture of gratitude.

By incorporating gratitude into our interactions with others, we contribute to stronger relationships and a more supportive social environment. The appreciation we express and the kindness we offer can have a lasting impact on those around us, creating a cycle of positivity and connection.

Conclusion

Cultivating gratitude is a transformative practice that can enhance our mental and physical well-being, strengthen relationships, and improve overall life satisfaction. By incorporating gratitude into our daily routines, we can shift our focus from what's lacking to what's abundant, fostering a more positive and fulfilling outlook on life.

Gratitude is not just a fleeting emotion but a way of life that can be nurtured and developed through intentional practices. Whether through journaling, mindful appreciation, or acts of kindness, the strategies outlined in this chapter offer practical ways to integrate gratitude into your life. As you embark on this journey, remember that cultivating gratitude is a continuous process that evolves over time. Embrace the practice with an open heart and mind, and witness the profound impact it can have on your life and the lives of those around you.

Chapter: 3 Embracing the Present Moment

In our fast-paced world, where the demands of daily life often pull us in multiple directions, it's easy to become preoccupied with the past or the future. We may find ourselves dwelling on past mistakes or anxiously anticipating future events, while the present moment slips through our fingers. Yet, the present moment is the only time we truly have, and learning to embrace it can profoundly transform our lives. This chapter explores the importance of living in the present, the benefits it brings, and practical strategies to help you fully experience and appreciate each moment.

The Essence of the Present Moment

To embrace the present moment means to be fully aware and engaged in the here and now. It involves letting go of distractions and judgments and focusing on the immediate experience. This concept is often associated with mindfulness, a practice rooted in various spiritual and philosophical traditions, including Buddhism and Stoicism.

Living in the present requires a conscious effort to let go of regrets about the past and worries about the future. It's about savouring the current experience, whether it's a routine activity or a significant event. When we embrace the present moment, we connect with life as it unfolds, rather than being caught up in mental narratives or external distractions.

The Benefits of Embracing the Present Moment

Embracing the present moment offers numerous benefits for our mental, emotional, and physical well-being. Here are some key advantages:

1. Reduced Stress: Focusing on the present moment can help alleviate stress by shifting attention away from future anxieties and past regrets. When we immerse ourselves in the here and now,

we're less likely to become overwhelmed by concerns about what might happen or what has already occurred.

2. Improved Mental Clarity: Being present enhances our ability to think clearly and make informed decisions. When we're not distracted by ruminations about the past or worries about the future, we can approach problems with a more focused and calm mindset.

3. Enhanced Emotional Well-Being: Embracing the present moment can lead to greater emotional stability and satisfaction. By fully experiencing and appreciating our current circumstances, we're more likely to find contentment and joy in everyday life.

4. Deeper Relationships:** When we are fully present in our interactions with others, we build stronger and more meaningful connections. Active listening and genuine engagement enhance our relationships and foster a greater sense of intimacy and understanding.

5. Increased Resilience: Living in the present moment can bolster our resilience in the face of challenges. By focusing on what we can control in the here and now, we're better equipped to navigate difficulties and adapt to changing circumstances.

6. Greater Enjoyment of Life: Embracing the present allows us to fully savor experiences and find pleasure in the small moments of daily life. Whether it's enjoying a meal, appreciating nature, or engaging in a hobby, being present enriches our experiences and adds depth to our enjoyment.

Practical Strategies for Embracing the Present Moment

Cultivating the ability to live in the present moment requires practice and intention. Here are some practical strategies to help you embrace the here and now:

1. Practice Mindfulness: Mindfulness involves paying deliberate attention to the present moment with openness and acceptance. You can practise mindfulness through various techniques, such as mindful breathing, body scans, or mindful eating. Start by dedicating a few minutes each day to mindfulness exercises and gradually incorporate them into your daily routine.

2. Engage Your Senses: Use your senses to ground yourself in the present moment. Pay attention to the sights, sounds, smells, tastes, and textures around you. Engaging your senses helps anchor your awareness to the here and now and can enhance your overall sensory experience.

3. Perform Single-Tasking: Multitasking can scatter our attention and detract from our ability to fully engage in the present moment. Instead, focus on one task at a time. Whether you're working, eating, or conversing with someone, give your full attention to the activity at hand.

4. Practice Gratitude: Gratitude can help shift your focus to the positives in your current experience. Regularly acknowledge and appreciate the things you're grateful for in the present moment. This practice can enhance your overall sense of well-being and help you stay grounded in the here and now.

5. Create Rituals of Presence: Incorporate rituals into your daily routine that encourage mindfulness and presence. For example, you might start each day with a brief meditation, take mindful breaks throughout the day, or end your evening with a reflection on the day's experiences.

6. Limit Distractions: Minimise distractions that pull you away from the present moment. This might involve setting boundaries with technology, creating a clutter-free environment, or establishing dedicated times for focused work or relaxation.

7. Cultivate Self-Awareness: Develop a greater awareness of your thoughts and emotions. When you notice yourself drifting into thoughts about the past or future, gently bring your focus back to the present moment. Self-awareness allows you to recognize when you're not fully present and take steps to refocus.

8. Embrace Acceptance: Accepting the present moment as it is, without judgement or resistance, is a key aspect of mindfulness. Let go of the need to control or change your current experience and instead, embrace it with an open and accepting attitude.

 Overcoming Challenges to Living in the Present

While the practice of embracing the present moment offers many benefits, it can also present challenges. Here are some common obstacles and strategies to overcome them:

1. Ruminating on the Past: Dwelling on past mistakes or missed opportunities can detract from your ability to be present. To overcome this, practice self-compassion and acknowledge that the past cannot be changed. Redirect your focus to the present moment and what you can do now.

2. Worrying About the Future: Anxiety about future events can prevent you from fully engaging in the present. To manage future-oriented worries, practice grounding techniques such as mindfulness or journaling. Focus on actionable steps you can take in the present to address your concerns.

3. Distraction from Technology: Constant notifications and digital distractions can pull you away from the present moment. Set boundaries for technology use, such as designated times for checking emails or social media, and create technology-free zones to help maintain your focus.

4. High-Stress Environments Stressful environments can make it difficult to stay present. In such situations, practise deep breathing

or mindfulness exercises to help center yourself. Creating a calming routine or finding moments of quiet can also aid in maintaining presence amidst chaos.

5. Difficulty in Slowing Down: In a culture that values productivity and speed, it can be challenging to slow down and embrace the present. Start by incorporating small moments of stillness into your day. Gradually increase these moments as you become more comfortable with slowing down.

The Ripple Effect of Embracing the Present Moment

Embracing the present moment not only benefits your own well-being but also has a positive impact on those around you. When you are fully present, you bring a sense of calm, attentiveness, and engagement to your interactions. This can foster deeper connections, enhance communication, and create a more supportive and mindful environment.

Additionally, living in the present moment can inspire others to do the same. By modelling mindfulness and presence, you contribute to a culture that values intentional living and meaningful connections. Your practice of embracing the here and now can create a ripple effect, encouraging others to explore and adopt similar practices in their own lives.

Conclusion

Embracing the present moment is a powerful practice that can transform your experience of life. By focusing on the here and now, you can reduce stress, enhance mental clarity, build stronger relationships, and find greater joy in everyday experiences. The journey to living in the present requires intention, practice, and self-awareness, but the rewards are profound.

As you embark on this journey, remember that embracing the present moment is an ongoing process. There will be times when you find yourself distracted or preoccupied with other thoughts, and that's okay. The key is to gently bring your focus back to the here and now and continue to cultivate a mindful and appreciative approach to life.

By incorporating mindfulness practices into your daily routine and embracing the present moment, you can unlock a deeper sense of fulfilment and connection. Life unfolds in the present, and by fully engaging with it, you can experience its richness and beauty in ways that are truly transformative.

Chapter: 4 The Art of Positive Affirmations

In a world where self-doubt and negative self-talk often prevail, positive affirmations offer a transformative tool for fostering a more optimistic and empowered mindset. Positive affirmations are simple, yet profound statements designed to reinforce positive beliefs and encourage constructive thinking. This chapter explores the essence of positive affirmations, their benefits, and practical strategies for crafting and using them effectively in your daily life.

Understanding Positive Affirmations

Positive affirmations are concise, positive statements that are repeated to oneself with the intention of shaping thought patterns, beliefs, and behaviours. They are rooted in the idea that our thoughts have the power to influence our reality. By consciously directing our thoughts toward positive outcomes, affirmations help rewire our subconscious mind and cultivate a more positive outlook.

The core principle behind affirmations is that our self-talk and internal dialogue can either uplift or undermine our sense of self-worth and potential. Positive affirmations act as a counterbalance to negative self-talk, offering a more constructive and empowering narrative. They are based on the belief that by affirming positive truths, we can foster self-confidence, resilience, and a sense of purpose.

The Benefits of Positive Affirmations

The practice of using positive affirmations offers numerous benefits for mental, emotional, and physical well-being. Here are some key advantages:

1. Enhanced Self-Esteem: Repeating positive affirmations can bolster self-esteem and self-confidence. By affirming your worth and abilities, you reinforce a positive self-image and counteract feelings of inadequacy.

2. Improved Mental Focus: Positive affirmations can help sharpen your focus and clarify your goals. By consistently affirming your intentions and aspirations, you create a mental framework that supports goal achievement and personal growth.

3. Stress Reduction: Affirmations can contribute to reduced stress levels by shifting your focus from negative thoughts and worries to positive, calming statements. This mental shift can promote relaxation and emotional balance.

4. Increased Resilience: Embracing positive affirmations can strengthen your resilience in the face of challenges. By reinforcing a positive mindset, you are better equipped to navigate obstacles and maintain a hopeful outlook.

5. Enhanced Motivation: Positive affirmations can serve as a source of motivation and encouragement. By affirming your goals and aspirations, you create a sense of purpose and drive that propels you toward success.

6. Greater Emotional Well-Being: Affirmations can elevate your mood and emotional state. By focusing on positive aspects of your

life and expressing gratitude, you cultivate a greater sense of happiness and contentment.

Crafting Effective Positive Affirmations

Creating effective positive affirmations involves more than simply stating positive phrases. To maximise their impact, consider the following guidelines:

1. Be Specific and Clear: Craft affirmations that are specific and clear, addressing particular aspects of your life or goals. Instead of vague statements like "I am successful," use more specific affirmations such as "I am achieving my career goals through hard work and dedication."

2. Use the Present Tense: Frame affirmations in the present tense, as if they are already true. This approach helps create a sense of immediacy and reinforces the belief that your goals and aspirations are already being realised. For example, say "I am confident and capable" rather than "I will be confident and capable."

3. Make Them Personal: Tailor affirmations to your own experiences and aspirations. Personal affirmations resonate more deeply and have a greater impact. Choose statements that reflect your values, desires, and unique qualities.

4. Ensure Positivity: Focus on positive and affirmative language. Avoid negative phrasing or statements that emphasise what you don't want. Instead of "I am not afraid," use "I am brave and confident."

5. Keep Them Short and Memorable: Craft affirmations that are concise and easy to remember. Short, memorable statements are easier to repeat and integrate into your daily routine. For instance, "I am worthy of love and success" is straightforward and impactful.

6. Include Emotional Resonance: Choose affirmations that evoke positive emotions and resonate with your personal experiences. Emotional resonance enhances the effectiveness of affirmations and helps them become more meaningful.

 Integrating Positive Affirmations into Daily Life

Incorporating positive affirmations into your daily routine can significantly enhance their impact. Here are some practical strategies for making affirmations a regular part of your life:

1. Morning Rituals: Begin your day with positive affirmations as part of your morning routine. Repeating affirmations while getting ready for the day or during your morning meditation can set a positive tone for the day ahead.

2. Affirmation Journals: Keep a journal dedicated to positive affirmations. Write down your affirmations daily, and reflect on their impact on your thoughts and behaviors. Journaling helps reinforce your affirmations and track your progress over time.

3. Visual Reminders: Place visual reminders of your affirmations in prominent locations, such as on your mirror, desk, or computer screen. Seeing these reminders regularly reinforces your positive statements and keeps them at the forefront of your mind.

4. Affirmation Apps: Utilise affirmation apps or digital tools that deliver daily affirmations to your phone or computer. These apps can provide a steady stream of positive reinforcement and help you stay consistent with your practice.

5. **Incorporate into Meditation:** Integrate affirmations into your meditation practice. During meditation, focus on your chosen affirmations and their positive effects. This approach deepens your connection to the affirmations and enhances their impact.

6. Affirmation Visualisation: Combine affirmations with visualisation techniques. As you repeat your affirmations, visualise yourself embodying the qualities or achieving the goals described in the statements. Visualisation helps create a mental image of success and reinforces the affirmations.

7. Share with Others: Share your affirmations with supportive friends or family members. Encouraging others to engage in positive affirmations can create a supportive environment and reinforce the practice in your own life.

Overcoming Challenges with Positive Affirmations

While positive affirmations can be a powerful tool, challenges may arise when incorporating them into your life. Here are some common obstacles and strategies to address them:

1. Scepticism: You may encounter scepticism or self-doubt regarding the effectiveness of affirmations. To overcome this, approach affirmations with an open mind and patience. Consistent practice and reflection on the positive changes you experience can help build confidence in their impact.

2. Resistance to Change: It may be challenging to shift deeply ingrained negative thought patterns. Start with affirmations that address specific areas of resistance and gradually build your practice. Consistent repetition and self-compassion can facilitate positive change over time.

3. Lack of Consistency: Maintaining a consistent practice of affirmations can be difficult. Establish a routine that integrates affirmations into your daily life, and use reminders or tools to help you stay on track. The key is persistence and regular practice.

4. Emotional Disconnection: At times, affirmations may feel disconnected from your current emotional state. If you experience resistance, acknowledge your feelings and gently reframe your

affirmations to align with your emotions. Practice self-compassion and allow yourself time to adjust.

5. Unrealistic Expectations: Be mindful of setting realistic expectations for the impact of affirmations. While affirmations can be transformative, they are one component of personal growth. Combine affirmations with other positive practices and actions to achieve your goals.

The Ripple Effect of Positive Affirmations

The practice of positive affirmations can create a ripple effect, influencing not only your own life but also the lives of those around you. By embodying positivity and self-confidence, you inspire others to adopt similar practices and contribute to a more supportive and empowering environment.

When you engage in positive affirmations, you set an example for friends, family, and colleagues. Your positive mindset and behaviours can encourage others to explore and embrace their own affirmations, fostering a culture of optimism and self-empowerment.

Conclusion

The art of positive affirmations lies in their simplicity and profound impact on our thoughts, beliefs, and behaviours. By crafting and integrating positive affirmations into our daily lives, we can enhance our self-esteem, reduce stress, and cultivate a more optimistic and empowered mindset.

Affirmations offer a powerful tool for reshaping our internal dialogue and fostering positive change. By approaching affirmations with intention, consistency, and emotional resonance, we can unlock their transformative potential and create a more fulfilling and empowered life.

As you embark on your journey with positive affirmations, remember that the practice is a dynamic and evolving process. Embrace the journey with patience and an open heart, and witness the positive shifts that unfold as you harness the art of affirmations to shape your reality and enhance your well-being.

Chapter: 5 Nurturing Relationships

Relationships are the cornerstone of human experience, providing us with emotional support, companionship, and a sense of belonging. Nurturing relationships, whether with family, friends, or romantic partners, requires conscious effort and intentional actions. This chapter delves into the importance of nurturing relationships, the benefits of strong connections, and practical strategies for cultivating and maintaining healthy and fulfilling relationships in your life.

The Importance of Nurturing Relationships

Nurturing relationships is not just about maintaining existing connections; it's about actively investing in and enriching these bonds. Strong relationships contribute to our overall well-being and happiness. They provide a sense of security, support during challenging times, and joy during moments of celebration. By nurturing relationships, we foster a network of positive connections that enhance our lives and provide a foundation for personal growth.

Here are some reasons why nurturing relationships is essential:

1. Emotional Support: Strong relationships offer emotional support during difficult times. Having someone to confide in and share your experiences with can alleviate stress and provide comfort.

2. Social Connection: Humans are inherently social beings. Meaningful relationships fulfil our need for connection and belonging, which is crucial for mental health and overall well-being.

3. Personal Growth: Relationships challenge us and provide opportunities for personal growth. Through interactions with others, we learn more about ourselves and develop essential skills such as empathy, communication, and problem-solving.

4. Increased Happiness: Positive relationships contribute to greater happiness and life satisfaction. Spending time with loved ones, sharing experiences, and building memories enhance our sense of joy and fulfilment.

5. Health Benefits: Strong social connections are associated with numerous health benefits, including lower risk of chronic diseases, improved immune function, and longer lifespan. Nurturing relationships can positively impact both mental and physical health.

Key Components of Healthy Relationships

Healthy relationships are built on several key components that contribute to their strength and longevity. These components include:

1. Communication, Open, honest, and respectful communication is fundamental to any healthy relationship. Effective communication involves active listening, expressing thoughts and feelings clearly, and addressing misunderstandings promptly.

2. Trust: Trust forms the foundation of a strong relationship. Building and maintaining trust requires consistency, reliability, and transparency. Trust is established over time through actions that demonstrate integrity and respect.

3. Respect: Mutual respect is essential for nurturing relationships. Respecting each other's boundaries, opinions, and individuality fosters a positive and supportive environment.

4. Empathy: Empathy involves understanding and sharing the feelings of another person. Practising empathy helps strengthen emotional connections and fosters a deeper sense of compassion and support.

5. Quality Time: Spending quality time together strengthens relationships and deepens connections. Engaging in shared activities, having meaningful conversations, and creating memories together contribute to relationship satisfaction.

6. Support: Providing and receiving support is crucial for nurturing relationships. Being there for each other during times of need and celebrating each other's successes fosters a sense of mutual care and encouragement.

7. Conflict Resolution: Conflicts are a natural part of any relationship. Effective conflict resolution involves addressing issues constructively, finding common ground, and working towards solutions that benefit both parties.

Practical Strategies for Nurturing Relationships

Nurturing relationships requires intentional actions and ongoing effort. Here are some practical strategies to help you cultivate and maintain strong and fulfilling connections:

1. Prioritise Relationships: Make relationships a priority in your life. Set aside time for family, friends, and partners, and be intentional about staying connected. Regularly reach out, schedule visits, and show appreciation for the people you care about.

2. Practise Active Listening: Practise active listening during conversations by giving your full attention and showing genuine interest in what the other person is saying. Avoid interrupting and respond thoughtfully to demonstrate that you value their perspective.

3. Express Appreciation: Regularly express gratitude and appreciation for the people in your life. Acknowledge their efforts, celebrate their achievements, and let them know how much they mean to you.

4. Be Present: When spending time with loved ones, be fully present and engaged. Put away distractions such as phones and focus on enjoying the moment together. Quality time is enhanced when you are attentive and involved.

5. Offer Support: Be a source of support and encouragement for those you care about. Offer a listening ear, provide practical help when needed, and celebrate their successes. Your support fosters a sense of security and trust.

6. Resolve Conflicts Constructively: Approach conflicts with a solution-oriented mindset. Address issues calmly and respectfully, and work towards finding mutually acceptable resolutions. Avoid

blaming or criticising, and focus on understanding each other's perspectives.

7. Create Shared Experiences: Engage in activities that bring you closer together and create positive memories. Whether it's exploring new hobbies, going on trips, or simply enjoying quality time together, shared experiences strengthen bonds and deepen connections.

8. Respect Boundaries: Recognize and respect each other's boundaries and personal space. Healthy relationships involve understanding and honouring each other's needs and limitations.

9. Show Empathy: Practise empathy by putting yourself in the other person's shoes and acknowledging their feelings. Offer comfort and support, and validate their experiences to strengthen emotional connections.

10. Foster Open Communication: Encourage open and honest communication by creating a safe space for sharing thoughts and feelings. Be receptive to feedback and address any concerns or misunderstandings openly.

Overcoming Challenges in Relationships

Maintaining strong relationships can be challenging, and conflicts or difficulties may arise. Here are some common challenges and strategies for overcoming them:

1. Miscommunication: Miscommunication can lead to misunderstandings and conflicts. To overcome this, clarify your messages, ask questions if something is unclear, and actively listen to ensure mutual understanding.

2. Busy Schedules: Busy schedules and competing priorities can strain relationships. To address this, prioritise quality time together,

schedule regular check-ins, and find creative ways to stay connected despite busy lives.

3. Different Expectations: Differences in expectations or goals can create tension. Openly discuss your expectations, align your goals, and work towards finding common ground that respects both parties' needs.

4. Unresolved Conflicts: Unresolved conflicts can fester and impact the relationship. Address issues promptly, seek resolution, and avoid holding grudges. Use conflict resolution strategies to address concerns constructively.

5. Distance or Separation: Physical distance or separation can challenge relationships. Stay connected through regular communication, virtual meetings, and planned visits. Focus on maintaining emotional closeness despite the physical distance.

6. Trust Issues: Rebuilding trust after a breach can be challenging. Approach the situation with honesty, patience, and commitment to rebuilding trust. Acknowledge past issues and demonstrate consistent behaviour to restore confidence.

7. Change and Growth: Personal growth and change can impact relationships. Embrace change with openness and adaptability, and support each other's growth. Communicate openly about evolving needs and aspirations.

The Ripple Effect of Nurturing Relationships

Nurturing relationships extends beyond individual connections; it has a ripple effect on the broader community. Strong relationships contribute to a more supportive and compassionate environment. By fostering positive interactions and meaningful connections, you inspire others to engage in similar practices and contribute to a culture of care and respect.

Nurturing relationships also sets a positive example for others, including family members, friends, and colleagues. Your commitment to cultivating strong connections encourages those around you to prioritise relationships and engage in meaningful interactions.

Conclusion

Nurturing relationships is an essential aspect of a fulfilling and meaningful life. By investing time, effort, and care into your connections with others, you build a network of support, joy, and personal growth. Healthy relationships provide emotional support, foster personal development, and enhance overall well-being.

The art of nurturing relationships involves effective communication, mutual respect, empathy, and a commitment to maintaining strong connections. By implementing practical strategies and addressing challenges with resilience and compassion, you can cultivate and sustain meaningful relationships that enrich your life and the lives of those around you.

As you embark on the journey of nurturing relationships, remember that it is a continuous process of growth and engagement. Embrace the opportunities for connection, celebrate the bonds you build, and contribute to a culture of support and positivity in your relationships. Through conscious effort and genuine care, you can create lasting and fulfilling connections that bring joy and meaning to your life.

Chapter: 6 Finding Joy in Creativity

Creativity is a powerful and transformative force that enriches our lives and adds meaning to our existence. It is not limited to artistic endeavours or professional achievements; rather, creativity permeates all aspects of life, offering a pathway to personal fulfilment, problem-solving, and self-expression. This chapter delves into the joy found in creativity, exploring its benefits, and providing practical strategies for cultivating and embracing your creative potential.

Understanding the Joy of Creativity

Creativity is often associated with the arts—painting, writing, music, and design—but its essence extends far beyond these realms. At its core, creativity involves the ability to think differently, explore new ideas, and bring something unique into the world. The joy of creativity lies in the process of creation itself, the satisfaction of seeing one's ideas come to life, and the personal growth that comes from engaging in creative activities.

Here are some fundamental aspects of the joy found in creativity:

1. Self-Expression: Creativity provides a means of expressing thoughts, emotions, and ideas that may be difficult to articulate otherwise. Whether through art, writing, or other forms of creation, expressing oneself creatively can be deeply fulfilling and empowering.

2. Exploration and Discovery: Engaging in creative activities often involves exploration and discovery. This process of experimentation and exploration allows individuals to uncover new perspectives,

solutions, and possibilities, contributing to a sense of wonder and excitement.

3. Flow State: Creativity often leads to a state of "flow," where individuals are fully immersed in the creative process and lose track of time. This state of focused engagement and enjoyment is inherently rewarding and can bring a profound sense of satisfaction and joy.

4. Personal Growth: Creative endeavours challenge individuals to step outside their comfort zones, take risks, and embrace uncertainty. This process fosters personal growth, resilience, and a greater understanding of oneself.

5. Connection and Sharing: Creativity can also facilitate connections with others. Sharing creative work with others, whether through exhibitions, performances, or collaborations, fosters a sense of community and connection.

6. Problem-Solving: Creativity is a powerful tool for problem-solving. The ability to think creatively allows individuals to approach challenges from different angles and find innovative solutions.

The Benefits of Embracing Creativity

Embracing creativity offers numerous benefits that extend beyond the joy of creation itself. These benefits include:

1. Enhanced Well-Being: Engaging in creative activities has been linked to improved mental health and overall well-being. Creative expression can reduce stress, increase feelings of happiness, and promote a positive outlook.

2. Increased Resilience: Creativity fosters resilience by encouraging individuals to approach challenges with a problem-solving mindset. The process of overcoming creative obstacles builds confidence and adaptability.

3. Improved Cognitive Function: Creative activities stimulate cognitive function by engaging different areas of the brain. This stimulation enhances critical thinking, problem-solving skills, and cognitive flexibility.

4. Greater Life Satisfaction: The fulfilment derived from creative endeavours contributes to greater life satisfaction. The sense of accomplishment and personal growth gained through creativity enhances overall happiness and fulfilment.

5. Strengthened Relationships: Creative collaborations and shared creative experiences strengthen relationships and build connections. Working on creative projects with others fosters teamwork, communication, and mutual support.

6. Increased Innovation: Creativity drives innovation and progress. By thinking outside the box and exploring new ideas, individuals and organisations can create novel solutions and advance their fields.

Practical Strategies for Cultivating Creativity

Cultivating creativity involves nurturing your creative potential and finding ways to integrate creative activities into your daily life. Here are some practical strategies to help you embrace and enhance your creativity:

1. Create a Creative Space: Designate a space that inspires and supports your creative activities. Whether it's a studio, a cosy corner, or a digital workspace, having a dedicated area for creativity can enhance focus and motivation.

2. Establish a Routine: Incorporate creative activities into your daily or weekly routine. Setting aside regular time for creative pursuits helps build a habit and ensures that creativity remains a consistent part of your life.

3. Experiment and Explore: Embrace experimentation and exploration in your creative endeavours. Try new techniques, mediums, or genres, and allow yourself to make mistakes and learn from them. Experimentation fosters innovation and growth.

4. Seek Inspiration: Surround yourself with sources of inspiration. This might include visiting art galleries, reading books, listening to music, or engaging with other creative works. Exposure to diverse ideas and perspectives can ignite your own creativity.

5. Collaborate with Others: Collaborate with others to gain new perspectives and ideas. Working on creative projects with friends, colleagues, or mentors can stimulate your creativity and lead to unexpected and exciting outcomes.

6. Practice Mindfulness: Mindfulness practices, such as meditation and deep breathing, can enhance creativity by promoting relaxation and mental clarity. A calm and focused mind is more receptive to creative ideas and insights.

7. Embrace Playfulness: Approach creative activities with a sense of playfulness and curiosity. Allow yourself to be spontaneous and enjoy the process of creation without rigid expectations or pressures.

8. Set Realistic Goals: Set achievable goals for your creative projects. Break larger projects into smaller, manageable tasks, and celebrate progress along the way. Realistic goals help maintain motivation and reduce feelings of overwhelm.

9. Reflect and Journal: Keep a journal to reflect on your creative process, ideas, and experiences. Journaling helps clarify your thoughts, track your progress, and identify patterns or insights that can inform future creative endeavours.

10. Take Breaks and Recharge: Avoid burnout by taking breaks and allowing yourself time to recharge. Stepping away from creative

work can provide fresh perspectives and renewed energy for your creative pursuits.

Overcoming Challenges in Creativity

While creativity offers immense joy and fulfilment, challenges may arise. Here are some common obstacles and strategies to overcome them:

1. Creative Block: Creative blocks can be frustrating and inhibit progress. To overcome a block, try changing your environment, taking a break, or engaging in different creative activities. Sometimes, stepping away and returning with a fresh perspective can help.

2. Self-Doubt: Self-doubt can undermine confidence and creativity. Address self-doubt by focusing on your strengths, seeking constructive feedback, and reminding yourself of past successes. Embrace a growth mindset and view challenges as opportunities for learning.

3. Perfectionism: Perfectionism can stifle creativity by creating unrealistic standards. Embrace the idea that imperfections are part of the creative process. Focus on progress rather than perfection and allow yourself to take creative risks.

4. Lack of Time: Busy schedules can limit opportunities for creative pursuits. Prioritise creativity by scheduling dedicated time for creative activities and finding ways to incorporate creativity into daily routines.

5. Fear of Judgment: Fear of judgement or criticism can inhibit creative expression. Reframe your perspective by focusing on personal satisfaction and growth rather than external validation. Embrace the idea that creativity is a personal journey.

6. Limited Resources: Limited resources, such as materials or tools, can be a barrier to creativity. Adapt by using available resources creatively, exploring alternative materials, or finding low-cost solutions.

The Ripple Effect of Creativity

The impact of creativity extends beyond individual experiences. By embracing and nurturing creativity, you contribute to a broader culture of innovation and expression. Creative endeavours inspire others, foster community engagement, and drive positive change.

Sharing your creative work with others can spark inspiration and encourage others to explore their own creative potential. Creative projects often have a ripple effect, influencing and enriching the lives of those who encounter them.

Conclusion

Finding joy in creativity involves embracing the process of creation, exploring new ideas, and nurturing your creative potential. Creativity offers profound personal fulfilment, enhances well-being, and contributes to a richer, more meaningful life. By incorporating practical strategies for cultivating creativity and addressing common challenges, you can unlock your creative potential and experience the joy that comes from self-expression and exploration.

As you embark on your creative journey, remember that creativity is a lifelong adventure. Embrace the process with curiosity, playfulness, and openness. Celebrate your achievements, learn from challenges, and continue to explore new possibilities. Through creativity, you can find joy, personal growth, and a deeper connection to yourself and the world around you.

Chapter:7 Self-Care

In the hustle and bustle of modern life, self-care often becomes a secondary priority, overshadowed by work, responsibilities, and the demands of daily life. However, self-care is not a luxury—it's a vital practice for maintaining physical, emotional, and mental well-being. This chapter explores the concept of self-care, its importance, and practical strategies for integrating self-care into your daily routine to enhance overall health and happiness.

Understanding Self-Care

Self-care refers to the intentional activities and practices that individuals engage in to maintain and improve their well-being. It encompasses a broad range of actions, from physical health practices to emotional and mental health strategies. The essence of self-care is recognizing and addressing your own needs, setting boundaries, and making time for activities that rejuvenate and sustain you.

Key components of self-care include:

1. Physical Health: Taking care of your body through nutrition, exercise, rest, and regular medical check-ups. Physical health is the

foundation of overall well-being and directly impacts how you feel and function in daily life.

2. Emotional Well-Being: Managing and expressing your emotions in a healthy way. This involves practices that support emotional balance, such as mindfulness, journaling, and seeking support when needed.

3. Mental Health: Engaging in activities that stimulate and challenge your mind while managing stress and mental fatigue. Mental health practices include learning new skills, setting goals, and engaging in hobbies.

4. Social Connections: Maintaining and nurturing relationships with others. Social support and positive interactions contribute to a sense of belonging and emotional resilience.

5. Personal Growth: Pursuing activities and goals that contribute to your personal development and fulfilment. This might include setting aspirations, exploring new interests, and reflecting on personal values and goals.

The Importance of Self-Care

Self-care is crucial for maintaining a balanced and healthy lifestyle. Here's why prioritising self-care matters:

1. Prevents Burnout: Regular self-care practices help prevent burnout by ensuring that you're not overwhelmed by stress and responsibilities. Taking time for yourself allows you to recharge and approach challenges with renewed energy.

2. Enhances Physical Health: Consistent self-care practices such as exercise, proper nutrition, and adequate rest contribute to better physical health, reducing the risk of illness and improving overall vitality.

3. Boosts Mental Health: Engaging in self-care supports mental health by reducing stress, managing anxiety, and enhancing mood. Practices such as mindfulness, relaxation techniques, and hobbies can alleviate symptoms of mental fatigue.

4. Strengthens Emotional Resilience: Self-care helps build emotional resilience by providing tools and strategies for managing emotions and coping with life's challenges. Emotional self-care practices promote self-awareness and emotional balance.

5. Improves Relationships: When you take care of yourself, you're better equipped to nurture and maintain healthy relationships. Self-care fosters self-awareness and personal growth, which positively impacts interactions with others.

6. Fosters Personal Fulfilment: Self-care allows you to pursue activities and goals that align with your values and passions. Engaging in personal interests and setting meaningful goals contributes to a sense of fulfilment and purpose.

Practical Strategies for Effective Self-Care

Integrating self-care into your daily routine involves identifying your needs and finding practices that work for you. Here are some practical strategies to help you incorporate self-care into your life:

1. Establish a Routine: Develop a self-care routine that includes daily, weekly, and monthly practices. Consistency is key to making self-care a habit and ensuring that it becomes an integral part of your life.

2. Prioritise Sleep: Ensure you get adequate rest each night. Establish a consistent sleep schedule, create a relaxing bedtime routine, and make your sleep environment comfortable to improve sleep quality.

3. Practice Mindfulness: Incorporate mindfulness practices such as meditation, deep breathing, or yoga into your routine. Mindfulness helps reduce stress, enhance focus, and promote emotional balance.

4. Engage in Physical Activity: Incorporate regular exercise into your routine, whether it's a daily walk, a workout session, or a recreational activity. Physical activity boosts energy levels, improves mood, and supports overall health.

5. Eat a Balanced Diet: Pay attention to your nutrition by consuming a balanced diet that includes a variety of fruits, vegetables, whole grains, and lean proteins. Proper nutrition supports physical health and energy levels.

6. Set Boundaries: Establish and maintain boundaries to protect your time and energy. Learn to say no when necessary, delegate tasks, and avoid overcommitting to prevent burnout and maintain balance.

7. Pursue Hobbies: Engage in activities that bring you joy and satisfaction. Whether it's reading, painting, gardening, or playing a musical instrument, pursuing hobbies provides a creative outlet and promotes personal fulfilment.

8. Connect with Others: Maintain and nurture social connections by spending time with friends and family. Social interactions provide emotional support, foster a sense of belonging, and enhance overall well-being.

9. Seek Professional Help: Don't hesitate to seek support from mental health professionals when needed. Therapy, counselling, or coaching can provide valuable insights and strategies for managing stress, anxiety, and other challenges.

10. Practice Gratitude: Incorporate gratitude practices into your routine, such as keeping a gratitude journal or regularly reflecting on

positive aspects of your life. Gratitude fosters a positive mindset and enhances emotional well-being.

11. Take Breaks: Allow yourself regular breaks throughout the day to rest and recharge. Short breaks can improve productivity, reduce stress, and prevent burnout.

12. **Engage in Relaxation:** Incorporate relaxation techniques such as taking baths, reading, or listening to calming music. Relaxation practices help alleviate stress and promote mental and emotional well-being.

Overcoming Challenges in Self-Care

While self-care is essential, it's not always easy to implement consistently. Here are some common challenges and strategies for overcoming them:

1. Time Constraints: Busy schedules can make it difficult to prioritise self-care. Address this challenge by scheduling dedicated self-care time, setting boundaries, and finding small ways to incorporate self-care into daily routines.

2. Guilt or Prioritization Issues: You may feel guilty about taking time for yourself or struggle to prioritise self-care. Reframe your perspective by recognizing that self-care is an investment in your overall well-being and effectiveness. Prioritising self-care ultimately benefits both yourself and others.

3. Lack of Motivation: Finding motivation for self-care can be challenging at times. Set achievable goals, celebrate small victories, and remind yourself of the positive impact self-care has on your well-being.

4. Financial Constraints: Some self-care practices may require financial resources, such as gym memberships or spa treatments.

Look for low-cost or free alternatives, such as home workouts, nature walks, or DIY relaxation techniques.

5. Resistance to Change: Incorporating new self-care practices may feel uncomfortable initially. Start with small, manageable changes and gradually build on them. Consistency and patience are key to establishing lasting self-care habits.

6. Health Issues: Physical or mental health challenges may impact your ability to engage in certain self-care practices. Adapt your self-care routine to accommodate your needs and consult with healthcare professionals for guidance.

The Ripple Effect of Self-Care

The benefits of self-care extend beyond individual well-being. By prioritising self-care, you contribute to a more positive and supportive environment for those around you. When you take care of yourself, you are better equipped to support and care for others, fostering a culture of mutual respect and well-being.

Self-care also sets a positive example for friends, family, and colleagues. By demonstrating the importance of self-care, you inspire others to prioritise their own well-being and create a ripple effect of positive change.

Conclusion

Self-care is an essential practice for maintaining physical, emotional, and mental well-being. By recognizing the importance of self-care and implementing practical strategies, you can enhance your overall health, prevent burnout, and experience greater fulfilment in your life.

Incorporating self-care into your daily routine involves making intentional choices and prioritising activities that support your well-being. Embrace the journey of self-care with compassion, consistency, and mindfulness. Remember that self-care is not a destination but an ongoing practice that evolves with your needs and circumstances.

As you cultivate a self-care routine, celebrate the positive impact it has on your life and the lives of those around you. By nurturing yourself, you foster a greater sense of balance, resilience, and joy, creating a foundation for a more fulfilling and meaningful life.

Chapter:8 Overcoming Challenges with a Positive Mindset

Challenges are an inevitable part of life, and how we respond to them can significantly impact our overall well-being and success. A positive mindset can transform obstacles into opportunities, turning adversity into a platform for growth and achievement. This chapter explores the power of a positive mindset in overcoming challenges, the benefits it offers, and practical strategies for cultivating and maintaining a positive outlook during difficult times.

The Power of a Positive Mindset

A positive mindset involves maintaining an optimistic and constructive attitude, even in the face of adversity. It is characterised by the ability to see possibilities rather than limitations, to approach problems with a solution-oriented mindset, and to maintain hope and resilience despite difficulties. Embracing a positive mindset can profoundly influence how you navigate challenges and shape your overall experience of life.

Here's why a positive mindset is powerful:

1. Enhances Resilience: positive mindset fosters resilience by helping you bounce back from setbacks and persist through difficulties. It encourages you to view challenges as temporary and surmountable rather than insurmountable barriers.

2. Improves Problem-Solving: When you approach challenges with a positive mindset, you are more likely to engage in creative problem-solving. Optimism opens the door to exploring various solutions and seeking innovative ways to overcome obstacles.

3. Boosts Emotional Well-Being: Positive thinking contributes to better emotional health by reducing stress, anxiety, and negative emotions. A positive mindset helps maintain a sense of hope and well-being even during tough times.

4. Strengthens Relationships: A positive outlook can positively impact your interactions with others. It fosters constructive communication, builds supportive relationships, and enhances your ability to collaborate effectively.

5. Increases Motivation: Maintaining a positive mindset fuels motivation and determination. Optimism encourages you to stay focused on your goals and take proactive steps toward achieving them, even in the face of challenges.

6. Promotes Physical Health: Research suggests that a positive mindset can positively influence physical health by reducing stress and improving overall well-being. Optimistic individuals often experience lower levels of chronic stress and better immune function.

Chapter 9 Cultivating a Positive Mindset

Developing and maintaining a positive mindset requires intentional practice and effort. Here are some practical strategies to help you cultivate a positive outlook:

1. Practice Gratitude: Regularly reflect on and acknowledge the things you are grateful for. Keeping a gratitude journal or taking a few moments each day to express appreciation for positive aspects of your life can shift your focus toward positivity.

2. Reframe Negative Thoughts: Challenge and reframe negative thoughts by replacing them with more positive or constructive alternatives. For example, instead of thinking, "I'll never be able to do this," reframe it as, "This is a challenge, but I can find a way to overcome it."

3. Set Realistic Goals: Break down larger challenges into smaller, manageable goals. Setting realistic and achievable objectives helps build confidence and provides a clear path forward, making it easier to maintain a positive mindset.

4. Surround Yourself with Positivity: Spend time with positive and supportive individuals who uplift and encourage you. Positive social interactions can reinforce your own optimistic outlook and provide a sense of encouragement and support.

5. Engage in Positive Self-Talk: Be mindful of the language you use when talking to yourself. Practise positive self-talk by affirming your strengths, acknowledging your efforts, and encouraging yourself during challenging times.

6. Practice Mindfulness: Mindfulness techniques, such as meditation and deep breathing, can help you stay present and manage stress. Mindfulness fosters a positive mindset by promoting self-awareness and reducing the impact of negative thoughts.

7. Celebrate Small Wins: Recognize and celebrate your progress and accomplishments, no matter how small. Celebrating achievements reinforces a sense of positivity and motivation, helping you stay focused on your goals.

8. Visualise Success: Use visualisation techniques to imagine yourself successfully overcoming challenges and achieving your goals. Visualisation can enhance your belief in your abilities and reinforce a positive outlook.

9. Seek Solutions, Not Blame: When faced with challenges, focus on finding solutions rather than dwelling on blame or past mistakes. A solution-oriented mindset encourages proactive problem-solving and maintains a positive focus.

10. Take Care of Yourself: Prioritise self-care to maintain physical and emotional well-being. Engage in activities that rejuvenate you, such as exercise, relaxation, and hobbies, to support a positive mindset.

Overcoming Common Challenges with a Positive Mindset

Different challenges require different approaches, but a positive mindset can be instrumental in overcoming various types of obstacles. Here's how to apply a positive mindset to common challenges:

1. Workplace Challenges: When facing difficulties at work, approach problems with a constructive mindset. Seek feedback, collaborate with colleagues, and focus on solutions rather than dwelling on

setbacks. Maintain a positive attitude and view challenges as opportunities for growth and development.

2. Personal Relationships: In challenging personal relationships, practice empathy, and open communication. Focus on understanding and addressing issues rather than assigning blame. A positive mindset helps foster constructive dialogue and strengthens connections.

3. Health Issues: When dealing with health challenges, maintain an optimistic outlook and focus on the steps you can take to improve your well-being. Adhere to medical advice, engage in healthy practices, and stay hopeful about recovery.

4. Financial Difficulties: Approach financial challenges with a positive and proactive mindset. Develop a budget, seek financial advice, and explore opportunities for improvement. Maintain hope and focus on long-term solutions rather than immediate frustrations.

5. Academic or Career Setbacks: In the face of academic or career setbacks, view failures as learning experiences and opportunities for growth. Set realistic goals, seek guidance, and stay motivated to pursue your objectives with resilience.

6. Personal Goals: When pursuing personal goals, such as learning a new skill or achieving a personal milestone, maintain a positive outlook even when progress seems slow. Celebrate small victories and stay focused on your long-term vision.

The Ripple Effect of a Positive Mindset

The impact of a positive mindset extends beyond personal challenges. By embracing and maintaining a positive outlook, you contribute to a more optimistic and supportive environment for others. Your positivity can inspire and uplift those around you, fostering a culture of encouragement and resilience.

A positive mindset also sets a powerful example for friends, family, and colleagues. By demonstrating how to approach challenges with optimism and constructive thinking, you encourage others to adopt similar attitudes and behaviours, creating a ripple effect of positivity and growth.

Conclusion

Overcoming challenges with a positive mindset is a transformative approach that can significantly impact your overall well-being and success. A positive mindset enhances resilience, improves problem-solving, boosts emotional well-being, and strengthens relationships. By cultivating and maintaining a positive outlook, you can navigate difficulties with greater ease, turning obstacles into opportunities for growth and achievement.

Integrating practical strategies for fostering a positive mindset, such as practising gratitude, reframing negative thoughts, and engaging in positive self-talk, can help you develop and sustain an optimistic outlook. Embrace challenges as opportunities for learning and growth, and maintain hope and resilience as you work towards your goals.

As you apply a positive mindset to your challenges, remember that your attitude shapes your experience and influences those around you. By fostering a positive outlook, you create a foundation for success, fulfilment, and a more hopeful and resilient life.

Chapter: 9 Creating a Joyful Environment

A joyful environment is more than just a pleasant space; it's a carefully curated atmosphere that fosters happiness, positivity, and well-being. Whether it's your home, workplace, or any other space you inhabit, creating an environment that nurtures joy can have profound effects on your overall quality of life. This chapter explores the principles and practices involved in crafting a joyful environment, providing practical strategies for transforming your surroundings into a space that uplifts and energises you.

Understanding the Joyful Environment

A joyful environment is characterised by elements that contribute to a sense of happiness, comfort, and positivity. It is a space where you feel relaxed, inspired, and connected. Creating such an environment involves thoughtful consideration of physical, emotional, and social factors that collectively contribute to a sense of well-being.

Here's why a joyful environment is important:

1 Enhances Well-Being: A joyful environment promotes emotional and psychological well-being by creating a space where you feel safe, valued, and inspired.

2. Boosts Productivity: In workspaces, a positive environment can enhance focus, creativity, and productivity. Employees who work in uplifting spaces are more likely to be engaged and motivated.

3. Strengthens Relationships: A joyful environment fosters positive interactions and strengthens relationships. It creates a welcoming atmosphere for social connections and collaboration.

4. Encourages Positive Habits: An environment designed for joy can support and encourage healthy habits, such as exercise, relaxation, and creativity.

5. Reduces Stress: A well-designed environment can mitigate stress and promote relaxation, contributing to overall mental and physical health.

Key Elements of a Joyful Environment

Creating a joyful environment involves integrating various elements that contribute to a sense of happiness and well-being. Here are some key components to consider:

1. Aesthetics and Design: The visual aspects of a space, including colour schemes, decor, and layout, play a crucial role in shaping its ambiance. Opt for colours and designs that evoke positive emotions and create a sense of harmony. Incorporate elements like natural light, plants, and art to enhance the overall aesthetic.

2. Comfort and Functionality: A joyful environment should be comfortable and functional. Invest in quality furniture, ensure proper lighting, and create spaces that cater to your needs. Comfort promotes relaxation and well-being, while functionality supports efficiency and ease of use.

3. Personal Touches: Infuse the space with personal touches that reflect your personality and preferences. Display meaningful items, such as photos, souvenirs, or artwork, to create a sense of connection and belonging.

4. Cleanliness and Organization: A clutter-free and well-organised space contributes to a sense of calm and order. Regularly declutter and organise your environment to maintain a clean and inviting atmosphere.

5. Positive Energy: Cultivate positive energy by incorporating elements that uplift and inspire. This could include uplifting quotes, calming music, or ambient scents that enhance the mood of the space.

6. Connection with Nature: Incorporating natural elements, such as plants, natural light, and outdoor views, can significantly enhance the joyfulness of a space. Nature has been shown to reduce stress and improve overall well-being.

7. Social and Recreational Spaces: Create areas designated for social interaction and recreation. Whether it's a cosy lounge area, a dining space, or a creative corner, having spaces for connection and enjoyment fosters a sense of community and joy.

Practical Strategies for Creating a Joyful Environment

Transforming your environment into a joyful space involves practical steps that align with your preferences and needs. Here are some actionable strategies:

1. Redesign Your Space: Start by assessing your current environment and identifying areas for improvement. Redesign or rearrange your space to enhance its functionality and aesthetics. Consider elements like furniture layout, colour schemes, and decor.

2. Incorporate Natural Elements: Bring nature indoors by adding plants, flowers, or natural materials. Plants not only improve air quality but also contribute to a sense of tranquillity and well-being.

3. Use Color Wisely: Choose colours that evoke positive emotions and align with the purpose of the space. For example, calming blues and greens work well in relaxation areas, while vibrant colours like yellow and orange can energise social spaces.

4. Create Zones: Designate specific areas for different activities. Create zones for relaxation, work, exercise, and socialising. Each zone should be tailored to its intended purpose, ensuring comfort and functionality.

5. Personalise Your Space: Add personal touches that reflect your individuality. Display items that have sentimental value or bring you joy, such as photos, artwork, or collectibles.

6. Maintain Cleanliness: Regularly clean and organise your space to keep it inviting and clutter-free. Establish routines for tidying up and maintaining order to create a pleasant environment.

7. Enhance Lighting: Utilise a mix of natural and artificial lighting to create a well-lit and inviting space. Adjustable lighting options, such as dimmers or task lights, can help set the mood and support various activities.

8. Add Comfort Elements: Invest in comfortable furnishings and accessories, such as cushions, throws, and ergonomic furniture. Comfort contributes to relaxation and enjoyment in your space.

9. Incorporate Sounds and Scents: Use calming or uplifting music to enhance the ambiance. Aromatherapy with essential oils or scented candles can also contribute to a positive atmosphere.

10. Encourage Social Interaction: Design spaces that facilitate social interaction and connection. Create areas for gathering, conversation, and shared activities to foster a sense of community and joy.

Overcoming Challenges in Creating a Joyful Environment

While creating a joyful environment is rewarding, it may come with challenges. Here are some common obstacles and strategies for overcoming them:

1. Limited Space: If you have limited space, focus on optimising what you have. Use multifunctional furniture, vertical storage solutions, and clever organisation to make the most of your space.

2. Budget Constraints: Creating a joyful environment doesn't require a large budget. Prioritise small changes and DIY projects, such as repurposing furniture, adding plants, or using budget-friendly decor.

3. Clutter Issues: Dealing with clutter can be challenging. Implement a decluttering routine, categorise items, and establish organisation systems to maintain a clean and orderly environment.

4. Personal Preferences: If you're creating a shared space, consider the preferences and needs of others. Find a balance between individual tastes and collective needs to ensure that everyone feels comfortable and happy.

5. Maintenance: Maintaining a joyful environment requires ongoing effort. Establish routines for cleaning, organising, and updating your space to ensure it continues to be a positive and uplifting place.

6. Emotional Attachment: Letting go of items with emotional significance can be difficult. Approach decluttering with compassion and focus on the benefits of a more organised and joyful space.

The Ripple Effect of a Joyful Environment

A joyful environment has a positive impact not only on yourself but also on those around you. When your surroundings foster happiness and well-being, they create a ripple effect that extends to family members, colleagues, and friends. A positive environment promotes healthy relationships, encourages collaboration, and contributes to a more supportive and uplifting community.

By creating a joyful environment, you set an example for others to follow, inspiring them to cultivate their own spaces of happiness and positivity. The collective impact of joyful environments can lead to a more harmonious and connected community.

Conclusion

Creating a joyful environment involves intentionality and thoughtful consideration of various elements that contribute to happiness and well-being. By focusing on aesthetics, comfort, personalization, and positive energy, you can transform your space into a place that uplifts and energises you.

Implement practical strategies to enhance your environment, such as incorporating natural elements, using colour wisely, and maintaining cleanliness. Address challenges with creative solutions and embrace the ongoing process of nurturing your space.

A joyful environment not only enhances your own well-being but also positively influences those around you. By cultivating spaces of happiness and positivity, you contribute to a more supportive and connected community, creating a ripple effect of joy and fulfilment.

As you embark on the journey of creating a joyful environment, remember that the process is as rewarding as the outcome. Embrace the opportunity to shape your surroundings into a space that reflects your values, fosters well-being, and enriches your life.

Chapter:10 Spreading Joy to Others

Joy is a powerful, contagious force that has the ability to transform not only our own lives but also the lives of those around us. The act of spreading joy is not only a way to brighten someone else's day but also a means of creating a more positive and connected world. This chapter delves into the art of spreading joy, exploring its benefits, methods, and the profound impact it can have on individuals and communities.

The Essence of Spreading Joy

Spreading joy involves sharing positivity, kindness, and uplifting experiences with others. It's about creating moments that foster happiness and well-being, whether through small acts of kindness, thoughtful gestures, or supportive interactions. The essence of spreading joy lies in the genuine desire to make a difference in someone else's life and to contribute to a more positive and compassionate world.

Here's why spreading joy is important:

1. Enhances Relationships: Acts of joy and kindness strengthen bonds and improve relationships. Positive interactions create a sense of connection and mutual appreciation, fostering deeper and more meaningful relationships.

2. Boosts Emotional Well-Being: Giving joy can enhance your own emotional well-being. The act of making others happy often leads to increased feelings of satisfaction, fulfilment, and purpose.

3. Creates a Ripple Effect: Joy is contagious. When you spread joy, you inspire others to do the same, creating a ripple effect of positivity that can reach far beyond your immediate interactions.

4. Promotes a Positive Environment:* Spreading joy contributes to a more supportive and uplifting environment, whether at home, in the workplace, or within the community. Positive environments foster collaboration, creativity, and resilience.

5. Alleviates Stress: Acts of kindness and joy can reduce stress and improve mental health. Engaging in activities that make others happy can provide a sense of relief and balance in your own life.

Practical Ways to Spread Joy

Spreading joy doesn't require grand gestures or elaborate plans. Simple, everyday actions can have a profound impact. Here are some practical ways to spread joy to others:

1. Practice Kindness: Small acts of kindness, such as offering a compliment, holding the door open for someone, or helping a neighbour, can bring joy to others and create a positive atmosphere.

2. Express Appreciation: Take the time to express gratitude and appreciation to those around you. A heartfelt thank-you note, a kind word, or acknowledging someone's efforts can make them feel valued and uplifted.

3. Share Your Talents: Use your skills and talents to bring joy to others. Whether it's baking treats, playing music, or offering advice, sharing your abilities can create meaningful and enjoyable experiences for others.

4. Volunteer Your Time: Contribute to your community by volunteering. Giving your time and energy to support a cause or

organisation can bring joy to those in need and create a sense of fulfilment for you.

5. Celebrate Milestones: Acknowledge and celebrate the achievements and milestones of others. Whether it's a birthday, promotion, or personal accomplishment, celebrating these moments shows support and brings joy to those involved.

6. Listen and Empathise: Offer a listening ear and show empathy to those who may be struggling. Sometimes, simply being present and understanding can provide comfort and uplift someone's spirits.

7. Share Positivity Online: Use social media and digital platforms to spread positive messages, uplifting stories, and encouraging words. Sharing joy online can reach a wide audience and inspire others to embrace positivity.

8. Organise Joyful Events: Plan and organise events that bring people together for fun and celebration. Whether it's a gathering, a themed party, or a community event, creating opportunities for people to connect and enjoy themselves can spread joy.

9. Create Joyful Spaces: Design your environment to be uplifting and positive. A joyful space can enhance the well-being of those who visit or interact with it, creating an atmosphere of happiness and relaxation.

10. Be a Source of Encouragement: Offer support and encouragement to those pursuing their goals or facing challenges. Your words of encouragement can boost their confidence and inspire them to keep moving forward.

The Benefits of Spreading Joy

The act of spreading joy not only benefits others but also has positive effects on your own well-being. Here's how spreading joy can be beneficial for you:

1. Enhances Your Mood: Engaging in acts of kindness and spreading joy often leads to increased feelings of happiness and satisfaction. The act of making others happy can lift your own spirits.

2. Strengthens Social Connections: Spreading joy fosters stronger social connections and relationships. Positive interactions create bonds of trust, appreciation, and mutual support.

3. Boosts Self-Esteem: Contributing to the happiness of others can enhance your own self-esteem and sense of purpose. It reinforces the idea that you have a positive impact on the lives of those around you.

4. Promotes Mental Health: Acts of kindness and spreading joy can reduce stress and improve mental health. Engaging in positive actions contributes to a more balanced and resilient mindset.

5. Creates a Sense of Fulfilment: The joy that comes from making a difference in someone else's life can provide a profound sense of fulfilment and purpose. It adds meaning to your own experiences and interactions.

Overcoming Barriers to Spreading Joy

While spreading joy is rewarding, it can come with challenges. Here's how to overcome common barriers:

1. Time Constraints: Busy schedules can make it challenging to find time for acts of kindness. Look for small, manageable ways to incorporate joy into your daily routine, such as sending a quick message or offering a compliment.

2. Financial Limitations: You don't need to spend money to spread joy. Simple, thoughtful gestures, like a heartfelt note or a supportive conversation, can have a significant impact without financial cost.

3. Personal Struggles: If you're dealing with personal challenges, it may be difficult to focus on spreading joy. Practice self-care and seek support to ensure that you're in a positive state of mind to share joy with others.

4. Differences in Preferences: People have different preferences and needs when it comes to receiving joy. Pay attention to the individual preferences of those around you and tailor your actions accordingly.

5. Resistance or Scepticism: Some people may be resistant to or sceptical of acts of kindness. Approach these situations with patience and understanding, and continue to spread joy in ways that align with your values.

The Ripple Effect of Spreading Joy

Spreading joy has a ripple effect that extends far beyond individual interactions. When you share positivity and kindness, you inspire others to do the same, creating a cycle of joy and support that can impact entire communities.

The ripple effect of joy can lead to:

1. Strengthened Communities: As individuals spread joy, it creates a more connected and supportive community. Positive interactions foster a sense of belonging and mutual support.

2. Increased Resilience: A culture of joy and kindness enhances collective resilience, helping individuals and communities navigate challenges with greater strength and optimism.

3. Enhanced Well-Being: The collective impact of spreading joy contributes to overall well-being, creating environments where individuals feel valued, supported, and uplifted.

4. Inspiration for Change: Joyful actions can inspire others to contribute to positive change and make a difference in their own ways. This can lead to a broader impact and a more compassionate society.

Conclusion

Spreading joy is a powerful and transformative practice that enhances relationships, boosts emotional well-being, and contributes to a positive environment. By engaging in acts of kindness, expressing appreciation, and creating opportunities for connection and celebration, you can make a meaningful difference in the lives of others and foster a more joyful world.

Incorporate practical strategies for spreading joy into your daily routine, and overcome barriers with creativity and resilience. Embrace the ripple effect of positivity and recognize the profound impact your actions can have on individuals and communities.

As you embark on the journey of spreading joy, remember that the act of bringing happiness to others also enriches your own life. Embrace the opportunity to create moments of joy, inspire positive change, and contribute to a more compassionate and connected world.

Chapter: 11 Embracing a Life of Joy

Living a life of joy is more than just experiencing fleeting moments of happiness; it's about cultivating a deep-seated, enduring sense of contentment and fulfilment. Embracing a life of joy involves adopting a mindset and lifestyle that prioritises positivity, gratitude, and meaningful experiences. This chapter explores the essence of living a joyful life, the benefits it offers, and practical steps to make joy a central part of your daily existence.

Understanding a Life of Joy

A life of joy is characterised by a consistent sense of happiness, satisfaction, and well-being. It's not merely about having good times or achieving external success, but about nurturing an inner sense of contentment and resilience regardless of external circumstances. Embracing a life of joy involves focusing on what truly matters, maintaining a positive outlook, and engaging in practices that enhance overall well-being.

Here's why embracing a life of joy is important:

1. Enhances Overall Well-Being: Joy contributes to both emotional and physical well-being, reducing stress, improving mood, and enhancing overall health.

2. Fosters Resilience: A joyful mindset helps you navigate life's challenges with optimism and perseverance, making it easier to bounce back from setbacks.

3. Strengthens Relationships: Joyful individuals often build stronger, more positive relationships, as their happiness and positivity foster connection and support.

4. Promotes Fulfilment: Living a life of joy involves pursuing what truly matters to you, leading to a sense of purpose and fulfilment.

5. Creates a Positive Impact: A joyful outlook can inspire and uplift those around you, creating a ripple effect of positivity and kindness.

Core Principles of Embracing a Life of Joy

To embrace a life of joy, it's essential to understand and integrate core principles that support lasting happiness and fulfilment. Here are some foundational principles:

1. Gratitude: Cultivating gratitude involves regularly reflecting on and appreciating the positive aspects of your life. Gratitude shifts your focus from what's lacking to what's present, enhancing your overall sense of joy.

2. Mindfulness: Being present in the moment and fully engaging in your experiences fosters a deeper connection to joy. Mindfulness helps you savour life's pleasures and reduce stress by focusing on the here and now.

3. Positive Relationships: Building and nurturing relationships with supportive and positive individuals contribute to a joyful life. Surrounding yourself with people who uplift and inspire you enhances your overall happiness.

4. Self-Care: Prioritising self-care is essential for maintaining joy. Taking care of your physical, emotional, and mental well-being ensures that you have the energy and resilience to embrace joy in your daily life.

5. Purpose and Passion: Engaging in activities and pursuits that align with your values and passions adds meaning and satisfaction to your life. Pursuing your passions fosters a sense of purpose and fulfilment.

6. Resilience: Developing resilience helps you navigate life's ups and downs with a positive outlook. Resilient individuals view challenges as opportunities for growth, maintaining their joy even in difficult times.

7. Generosity: Acts of kindness and generosity not only benefit others but also enhance your own sense of joy. Contributing to the well-being of others creates a sense of connection and fulfilment.

Practical Steps to Embrace a Life of Joy

Embracing a life of joy involves integrating practices and habits into your daily routine that support happiness and well-being. Here are practical steps to cultivate a joyful life:

1. Start a Gratitude Journal: Set aside time each day to write down things you are grateful for. Reflecting on positive aspects of your life can shift your focus and enhance your sense of joy.

2. Practice Mindfulness: Incorporate mindfulness practices, such as meditation or deep breathing exercises, into your daily routine. Mindfulness helps you stay present and appreciate life's moments.

3. Foster Positive Relationships: Invest time and energy in building and maintaining positive relationships. Engage in activities with loved ones, communicate openly, and offer support to strengthen your connections.

4. Engage in Self-Care: Prioritise self-care activities that nurture your well-being, such as exercise, healthy eating, adequate rest, and relaxation. Taking care of yourself ensures that you have the physical and emotional resources to embrace joy.

5. Pursue Your Passions: Identify activities and goals that align with your passions and values. Dedicate time to pursuing these interests, whether through hobbies, creative projects, or professional aspirations.

6. Develop Resilience:* Build resilience by reframing challenges as opportunities for growth and learning. Practice problem-solving and seek support when needed to maintain a positive outlook.

7. Be Generous: Engage in acts of kindness and generosity, both big and small. Volunteer your time, offer support to others, and perform random acts of kindness to spread joy and create a positive impact.

8. Create Joyful Rituals: Establish rituals and routines that bring you joy and satisfaction. Whether it's a weekly family dinner, a morning walk, or a creative hobby, incorporating joyful rituals into your life enhances your overall sense of happiness.

9. Set Joyful Goals: Set goals that focus on enhancing your well-being and happiness. Align your objectives with activities and experiences that bring you joy and fulfilment.

10. Reflect and Adjust: Regularly reflect on your life and assess what brings you joy. Make adjustments as needed to ensure that your daily life aligns with your values and contributes to your overall happiness.

Overcoming Obstacles to Joy

Embracing a life of joy can come with challenges and obstacles. Here's how to address common barriers:

1. Negative Mindset: Combat negative thinking by practising positive self-talk and reframing challenges as opportunities. Focus on solutions rather than dwelling on problems.

2. Busy Schedule: Make time for activities that bring you joy, even within a busy schedule. Prioritise self-care and joyful practices to maintain a sense of balance and fulfilment.

3. Unresolved Issues: Address unresolved emotional or personal issues that may hinder your ability to experience joy. Seek support from professionals or engage in self-reflection and healing practices.

4. External Stressors: Manage external stressors, such as work or financial pressures, by implementing stress-reducing techniques and seeking support. Maintaining a positive outlook can help you navigate challenges with resilience.

5. Comparison to Others: Avoid comparing yourself to others and focus on your own journey and achievements. Embrace your unique path and celebrate your individual progress and successes.

The Ripple Effect of Embracing Joy

When you embrace a life of joy, the benefits extend beyond your own well-being. Your positive outlook and actions can inspire and uplift those around you, creating a ripple effect of happiness and positivity. Joyful individuals often contribute to a more supportive and compassionate community, fostering connection and goodwill.

The ripple effect of joy can lead to:

1. Stronger Communities: As individuals embrace joy, they contribute to a more connected and supportive community. Positive interactions and acts of kindness strengthen communal bonds and create a sense of belonging.

2. Enhanced Well-Being: The collective impact of joy improves the overall well-being of individuals and groups. A joyful environment fosters mental, emotional, and physical health, benefiting everyone involved.

3. Inspiration for Change: Embracing joy can inspire others to adopt a similar mindset and pursue their own paths to happiness. This inspiration can lead to positive changes and contributions to society.

4. Positive Influence: Your joy can influence and uplift those around you, creating a ripple effect that extends beyond your immediate circle. By sharing your happiness and positivity, you contribute to a more joyful and compassionate world.

Conclusion

Embracing a life of joy involves more than just seeking moments of happiness; it's about integrating joy into every aspect of your life. By focusing on core principles such as gratitude, mindfulness, positive relationships, and self-care, you can cultivate a deep-seated sense of fulfilment and well-being.

Implement practical steps to nurture joy in your daily routine, and address challenges with resilience and positivity. Recognize the ripple effect of your actions and embrace the opportunity to inspire and uplift others.

As you embark on the journey of embracing a life of joy, remember that joy is both a destination and a journey. It's about finding happiness in the present moment, pursuing what matters to you, and creating a positive impact on the world around you. Embrace the process with an open heart and a positive outlook, and enjoy the transformative power of living a joyful life.

Daily Reflection Worksheets: Guided Prompts for Journaling Your Thoughts and Tracking Your Progress

---

Daily reflection is a powerful practice that can help you gain insights into your thoughts, emotions, and experiences, fostering personal growth and well-being. Using guided prompts for journaling can structure your reflections, making it easier to track progress, set goals, and understand patterns in your life. Below are worksheets with prompts designed to help you engage in meaningful daily reflection.

Daily Reflection Worksheet

Date: _____

---

1. Morning Intentions:

    - What are your intentions or goals for today?
      Write down what you hope to achieve or focus on today.

    - How do you want to feel by the end of the day?
      *Describe the emotions or states of mind you wish to cultivate.

2. Gratitude Check-In:

   - What are three things you are grateful for today?
     List specific things, people, or experiences that you appreciate.

   - How did these things contribute to your overall sense of well-being?
     Reflect on how these aspects positively impact your day.

---

3. Mindfulness and Awareness:

   -What moment or experience today made you feel most present?
     Describe a moment when you were fully engaged and aware.

   - Were there any challenges to staying present? How did you handle them?
     Reflect on any difficulties with mindfulness and your response.*

4. Achievements and Progress:

   - What was your most significant accomplishment today?
     Highlight something you achieved or made progress on.
   - What did you learn from this experience?
     Consider any lessons or insights gained.

---

5. Emotional Reflection:**

   - What emotions did you experience today?
     List and describe the main emotions you felt throughout the day.

   - What triggered these emotions and how did you respond?

Reflect on the causes of your emotions and your reactions.

---

6. Acts of Kindness:

   - Did you perform or witness any acts of kindness today?
     Describe any acts of kindness you were involved in or observed.

   - How did these acts impact you or others?
     Reflect on the effects of these acts on yourself and those around you.

7. Reflection on Challenges:

   - What challenges or obstacles did you face today?

Identify any difficulties or setbacks you encountered.

   - How did you address or overcome these challenges?
     Describe your approach or strategies for dealing with these issues.

---

8. Evening Review:

   - What went well today?
     Summarise the positive aspects and successes of the day.

   - What could have gone better?
     Reflect on areas where improvements could be made.

   - What will you do differently tomorrow based on today's experiences?

*Consider any changes or adjustments you want to make for the future.

9. Self-Care Assessment:

   - How did you take care of yourself today?
     Describe any self-care activities or practices you engaged in.

   - What additional self-care might you need tomorrow?
     Identify any further self-care needs or practices for the following day.

10. Positive Affirmations:

    - Write down a positive affirmation or mantra for yourself:
      Create a statement that inspires and motivates you.

    - How does this affirmation reflect your goals and values?
      Explain how this affirmation aligns with what you want to achieve or embody.

---

11. Looking Forward:

    - What are you most looking forward to tomorrow?
      Identify something you are excited about or anticipate.

    - What steps can you take to ensure a positive day tomorrow?
      Plan any actions or attitudes that will help you have a fulfilling day.

Additional Tips for Using Your Reflection Worksheet

Consistency: Aim to complete your reflection worksheet at the same time each day to establish a routine. Morning reflections can set a positive tone for the day, while evening reflections can help you process and wind down.

- Be Honest: Approach your reflections with honesty and self-compassion. The goal is to understand yourself better, not to judge or criticise.

- Track Patterns: Over time, review your reflections to identify patterns in your emotions, challenges, and successes. This can provide valuable insights into your personal growth and areas for improvement.

- Celebrate Achievements* Take time to acknowledge and celebrate your accomplishments, no matter how small. Recognizing your progress can boost motivation and self-esteem.

- Adjust as Needed: Feel free to adapt the prompts to better suit your needs or preferences. The worksheet is a tool to support your personal growth, so make it work for you.

By regularly engaging in these guided reflections, you'll gain a deeper understanding of yourself, track your progress, and foster a more positive and intentional approach to life.

Resource List: Recommended Books, Apps, and Websites for Further Exploration of Positive Thinking and Happiness

Exploring positive thinking and happiness can be greatly enhanced with the right resources. Below is a curated list of books, apps, and websites that offer valuable insights, tools, and techniques to help you deepen your understanding and practice of positive thinking and well-being.

Books

1. "The Power of Now: A Guide to Spiritual Enlightenment" by Eckhart Tolle
   - Overview: This transformative book explores the importance of living in the present moment and offers practical guidance for achieving a state of mindfulness and inner peace.
   - *Why Read: It provides profound insights into overcoming negative thinking patterns and embracing a more joyful, present-focused life.

2. "The Happiness Project" by Gretchen Rubin
   - Overview:* Rubin chronicles her year-long experiment to increase her own happiness through practical, actionable strategies.
   - Why Read:* The book is filled with research-backed advice and real-life applications for boosting happiness.

3. "Feeling Good: The New Mood Therapy" by David D. Burns
   - Overview: Dr. Burns provides a comprehensive guide to cognitive behavioural therapy (CBT) techniques for overcoming depression and negative thinking.
   - Why Read: This book offers practical tools to reframe negative thoughts and develop a more positive mindset.

4. "The Four Agreements: A Practical Guide to Personal Freedom" by Don Miguel Ruiz
   - Overview: Ruiz presents four principles for personal development and emotional freedom that can lead to greater happiness and fulfilment.
   - Why Read: The agreements offer simple yet powerful guidelines for living a joyful and authentic life.

5. "Daring Greatly: How the Courage to Be Vulnerable Transforms the Way We Live, Love, Parent, and Lead" by Brené Brown**
   - Overview: Brown explores the concept of vulnerability and its role in fostering deeper connections and greater happiness.
   - Why Read: It provides insights into building resilience and embracing imperfections as a path to joy and fulfilment.

6. "The Gifts of Imperfection: Let Go of Who You Think You're Supposed to Be and Embrace Who You Are" by Brené Brown
   - Overview: This book encourages readers to embrace their authentic selves and let go of perfectionism to live a more joyful and meaningful life.
   - Why Read: It offers practical advice on cultivating self-compassion and embracing vulnerability.

7. "Atomic Habits: An Easy & Proven Way to Build Good Habits & Break Bad Ones" by James Clear
   - Overview: Clear provides a framework for building positive habits and making lasting changes to improve various aspects of your life.
   - Why Read: It offers actionable strategies for creating habits that enhance well-being and support a positive mindset.

Apps

1. Headspace
   - Overview: Headspace offers guided meditations and mindfulness exercises designed to reduce stress, enhance focus, and promote overall well-being.
   - Features: Daily meditations, sleep aids, and mindfulness exercises.
   - Platform: iOS, Android

2. Calm

- Overview: Calm provides a range of meditation, relaxation, and sleep resources to help users manage stress and enhance mental clarity.
   - Features: Guided meditations, sleep stories, breathing exercises, and relaxing music.
   - Platform: iOS, Android

3. Happify
   -*Overview: Happify uses science-based activities and games to help users improve their mood and overall happiness.
   -Features: Interactive activities, tracks for different aspects of well-being, and progress tracking.
   - Platform: iOS, Android

4. Moodfit
   - Overview: Moodfit is a comprehensive mental health app that offers tools for tracking mood, setting goals, and engaging in exercises to improve mental well-being.
   - Features: Mood tracking, gratitude journal, goal setting, and cognitive behavioural therapy (CBT) tools.
   -Platform: iOS, Android

5. Insight Timer
   - Overview: Insight Timer provides a vast library of guided meditations, music tracks, and talks from experts in mindfulness and well-being.
   - Features: Guided meditations, music, talks, and a meditation timer.
   - Platform: iOS, Android

6. Simple Habit
   - Overview: Simple Habit offers short, guided meditations to help users manage stress and improve mental clarity.
   - Features: Meditations for different situations, daily mindfulness exercises, and sleep aids.
   - Platform: iOS, Android

7. Gratitude Journal by Happyify
   - Overview: This app focuses on fostering gratitude by encouraging daily reflections and positive affirmations.
   - Features: Daily gratitude prompts, positive affirmations, and mood tracking.
   - Platform: iOS, Android

Websites

1. Positive Psychology Program (positivepsychology.com)
   - Overview: This website offers resources, articles, and tools on positive psychology, including exercises and techniques to enhance well-being.
   - Features: Articles, research summaries, practical exercises, and online courses.

2. Mindful ([mindful.org](https://www.mindful.org))
   - Overview: Mindful provides resources and articles on mindfulness and meditation practices to help cultivate a mindful approach to life.
   - Features: Articles, guided meditations, and mindfulness tips.

3. Greater Good Science Center(greatergood.berkeley.edu)
   - Overview: Hosted by the University of California, Berkeley, this site offers research-based insights and practical tips on happiness, gratitude, and well-being.
   - Features: Articles, research summaries, and online courses.

4. Happiness Studies Academy (happinessstudies.academy)

- Overview: This site offers courses and resources focused on the science of happiness and practical strategies for enhancing well-being.
   - Features: Online courses, articles, and research on happiness and well-being.

5. The Positivity Blog ([positivityblog.com](https://www.positivityblog.com))
   - Overview: This blog provides practical advice and strategies for fostering a positive mindset and living a happier life.
   - Features: Articles, tips, and personal development advice.

6. Tiny Buddha (tinybuddha.com)
   - Overview: Tiny Buddha offers articles, quotes, and resources on mindfulness, personal growth, and happiness.
   - Features: Articles, community forums, and inspirational content.

7. The Chopra Center (chopra.com)
   - Overview: Founded by Deepak Chopra, this site provides resources and programs focused on well-being, mindfulness, and spiritual growth.
   - Features: Articles, guided meditations, and wellness programs.

These resources offer a wealth of information and tools to support your journey toward positive thinking and increased happiness. Whether you prefer reading insightful books, using helpful apps, or exploring informative websites, these options can provide valuable guidance and support as you cultivate a more joyful and fulfilling life.

Inspirational Quotes to Uplift and Inspire Your Journey to a Joyful Life

Quotes have the power to inspire, motivate, and uplift us. They often encapsulate profound truths in a few words, providing wisdom and encouragement. Here is a collection of inspirational quotes to guide and inspire you on your journey to a joyful life.

On Joy and Happiness

1. "Happiness is not something ready-made. It comes from your own actions."
 — Dalai Lama

2. "The purpose of life is not to be happy. It is to be useful, to be honourable, to be compassionate, to have it make some difference that you have lived and lived well."
 — Ralph Waldo Emerson

3. "Joy is not in things; it is in us.
 — Richard Wagner

4. "For every minute you are angry you lose sixty seconds of happiness."
 — Ralph Waldo Emerson

5. "Happiness often sneaks in through a door you didn't know you left open."
 — John Barrymore

---

*On Positive Thinking

1. "The only limit to our realisation of tomorrow is our doubts of today."
 — Franklin D. Roosevelt

2. "The pessimist sees difficulty in every opportunity. The optimist sees opportunity in every difficulty."
 — Winston Churchill

3. "You have within you right now, everything you need to deal with whatever the world can throw at you."
  — Brian Tracy

4. You are never too old to set another goal or to dream a new dream."
  — C.S. Lewis

5. "In the middle of difficulty lies opportunity."
  — Albert Einstein

On Gratitude

1. "Gratitude turns what we have into enough."
  — Anonymous

2. "When we focus on our gratitude, the tide of disappointment goes out and the tide of love rushes in."
  — Anonymous

3. "Feeling gratitude and not expressing it is like wrapping a present and not giving it."
  — William Arthur Ward

4. "Gratitude is not only the greatest of virtues but the parent of all the others."
  — Cicero

5. "The more you practise the art of thankfulness, the more you have to be thankful for."
  — Anonymous

On Self-Care

1. "You yourself, as much as anybody in the entire universe, deserve your love and affection."
   — Buddha
2. "Self-care is not selfish. You cannot serve from an empty vessel."
   — Eleanor Brownn

3. "Almost everything will work again if you unplug it for a few minutes, including you."
   — Anne Lamott

4. "To love oneself is the beginning of a lifelong romance."
   — Oscar Wilde

5. "Taking care of yourself doesn't mean me first. It means me too."
   — L.R. Knost

On Overcoming Challenges

1. "Our greatest glory is not in never falling, but in rising every time we fall."
   — Confucius

2. "It does not matter how slowly you go as long as you do not stop."
   — Confucius

3. "Difficulties in life are intended to make us better, not bitter."
   — Anonymous

4. "The best way out is always through."
   — Robert Frost

5. "The only way to make sense out of change is to plunge into it, move with it, and join the dance."

— *Alan Watts*

On Living Fully

1. "Life is what happens when you're busy making other plans."
   — John Lennon

2. "The biggest adventure you can take is to live the life of your dreams."
   — Oprah Winfrey

3. "Do not follow where the path may lead. Go instead where there is no path and leave a trail."
   — Ralph Waldo Emerson

4. "The future belongs to those who believe in the beauty of their dreams."
   — Eleanor Roosevelt

5. "Life isn't about waiting for the storm to pass; it's about learning how to dance in the rain."
   — Vivian Greene

On Inner Strength

1. "You never know how strong you are until being strong is your only choice."
   — Bob Marley

2. "Believe you can and you're halfway there."
   — Theodore Roosevelt

3. "Strength does not come from physical capacity. It comes from an indomitable will."
   — Mahatma Gandhi

4. "It is not the mountain we conquer but ourselves."
   — Sir Edmund Hillary

5. "With the new day comes new strength and new thoughts."
   — Eleanor Roosevelt

These quotes are meant to inspire and uplift you as you navigate your journey toward a joyful and fulfilling life. Use them as daily reminders to stay positive, embrace gratitude, and maintain resilience.

Printed in Great Britain
by Amazon